PARTLY PANDE-MONIUM, PARTLY LOVE

PARTLY PANDE-MONIUM, PARTLY LOVE

POEMS BY MERRILL LEFFLER

D

Dryad Press

Washington, D.C. & San Francisco

Partly Pandemonium, Partly Love
Copyright © 1982 by Merrill Leffler.
Printed in the United States of America.

Acknowledgements

A number of these poems have appeared in the following magazines
and anthologies, some of them in altered forms.
Aleph, Calvert Review, City Celebration 1976 edited by Octave
Stevenson, *Dryad, The Poet Upstairs* © 1979 Washington Writer's
Publishing House, *Poetry Now, Positively Prince Street* © 1979
Positively Prince St., Inc., *Takoma Park Writers* © 1981 Suzanne
Rhodenbaugh, *The Unicorn and the Garden* © 1978 Betty Parry,
Visions, The Washington Star.

This project is supported by a grant from the National Endowment
for the Arts, a Federal agency. It was typeset at The Writer's
Center which is partially funded by a grant from the National
Endowment for the Arts and The Maryland Arts Council.

Library of Congress Catalogue Card Number: 82-70051
ISBN: 0-931848-46-6 (cloth); 0-931848-50-4 (paper)

Published by

Dryad Press

15 Sherman Avenue
Takoma Park, Maryland 20912

P.O. Box 29161 Presidio
San Francisco, California 94129

For the memory
of my mother and father

Ida Teitelbaum Leffler
and
Lew K. Leffler

Contents

I

"Instead of breaking the back of a willing phrase
why not try to follow the wheel through—approach
death at a walk, take in all the scenery."
                    —*Kora in Hell*

A Short History

Listen—
do you hear the music
in the earth that
makes us run? Of
birth and death
and inbetween the little
violences lifting their
scarred hands
in one poor truce after another

A Parable With No Justifiable Meaning

The lady had thin
yellow hair. She
walked with a limp
and could hardly bear
the sun and so hid from
the man with balloons
who had
a wide toothy
masculine grin
who
were truth known
was one
of the demons
of air. Of fair
complexion he
a bit opaque, biceps
like brick, an engineer
counting
his data by two's
then by three's,
divided
by the square root
of whatever
agrees.

And this
may sound silly
to you but it
wasn't at all
to the lady with thin
yellow hair
who died
of exposure
not from the sun
but the leer
of the man

with the wide toothy
grin and biceps
like brick
who walked on the beach
with balloons
in the air
and grinned at the lady
with yellowy hair
who
knew not enough
to get up
and scoot away
quick like a fish
out of there.

Beached

You all know him. His name is Jerry or Big John or Louie.
He lives in your house, he drives your car, slaps you on the
back at parties, is smoking a Havana cigar on the Fourth
of July, his hand is always shaking yours. He is the man
Theophrastus could pin wriggling on the wall. He is your
father, our uncle, a 32nd degree Mason or Pythian Knight;
he has a belly so round that when he lies down he is a
Mount Everest in the kingdom of ants. When he says to
noone in particular, "good morning" or "howareya" he
has entered stage left; when he walks down the street with
his divorced thirty year old son, the lifeguard in Miami he
looks for someone to say, "This is my kid brother—just
come in yesterday and already he's running downtown.
What'ar ya gonna do with these kids," cuffing the younger
neck with the anguish of affection. You have seen him in
television ads—when he opens his medicine chest in the
morning he pulls out Lavoris or Lysol; under his arms he
rolls Tickle and slaps Mennen on the skingoneleathery.
                                                    He
is someone else. OK. He is not you, friend, and he is not
me. I know that. But when he exits stage right and goes
home and the door closes behind him and he is in his under-
wear and cannot sleep; when he takes out a bicarbonate of
soda, when he pulls down his son's marriage album one
more time, when he remembers if only for an instant how
he went one glorious afternoon for candy with coins his
father once put in his palm, when he sees all the past as a
dark light hardly visible, when he tries to bring back the
past into the yellow light of his memory and has only snap
shots, tell me he is a twentieth century caricature. Tell me
that the poor drift of the darkening years of this most
modern of centuries hasn't beached its souls on their
passage. Tell me friend he is not you and that we will
still rescue the night from oblivion.

Grandfather and America

You may or may not be interested in this. It is for my son
who is far too young. At fifteen he may be interested and
by thirty, obsessed. After that I won't predict unless he has
children of his own. Then he will love this story and will
feel grief for its incompleteness, for the hole that will be
there when he needs to step backwards. My story has lost
its beginning. There is my grandfather, erect, severe thin
lips, and one blue eye, the other glass. With wet rags he is
reaching into the fireplace, carefully taking from the wall
hot bricks; the fire flames and spits, the heat drenching
his body. My uncle—a young boy of twelve—takes each
brick from his hand, stacking them neatly; one of the
daughters, my eldest aunt, hands my grandfather, separate-
ly, three metal plates, counterfeit government stamps
which, with the precision of a craftsman and the mind
of a forger, he has engraved (why? out of conviction? for
money?) and which he carefully places into the recess, my
uncle handing each brick back ("oh was he prepared" my
uncle grinned, telling me this years later), my grandfather's
shirt drenched in sweat returning each brick with the loving
care of achievement or victory I don't know. And asking
for schnaps, swallows quickly and goes silently into his
room, returning dry with new collar and tie, his suit jacket
buttoned and sitting down—his glass eye steady—for the
sabbath dinner, recited mechanically the blessing for bread
and gave his daughters and one son permission to eat.

Now
I can imagine—whether true or not—the clear yellow soup,
the white smoked fish, the red carp and herring in cream,
rich cheeses, black pumpernickel, cakes and tea with lumps
of sugar. And tight thin lips that I remember in his old
age and the silence he seemed to require. Who were the
authorities? In what year exactly did this occur? Was this
before Kerensky sat high on his snow white stallion
outside his shop, shouting, "Gospodjyn Teitelbaum"?
Where was my grandmother? What did she do? Where
were the other children? How much did they understand?
What danger was the family in? Questions I never asked—
I was not yet greedy enough.

And now when I have need
to know, they are all of them dead. There is this story
(and others as incomplete), in that house, in eastern
Poland, sometime before 1922. Is there any sadness like
being unable to call back a friend who is dead, whom you
never loved as you should have? And you live with that
hole in your memory which is like a hole in you. And what
there is to remember is the old man, silence as if sewn on
his lips, refusing until the end—another story goes—com-
ing to this wonderful America where the future waited.
And coming, against his will, said no to her fortunes, her
language, and sat at his bench and engraved trinkets or
in an armchair as if imprisoned, his one free eye looking
at television, I remember once, astonished at a schvartze
singing, and shaking his head in disbelief, and shaking his
head with the only strength I ever knew him by.

A Reply

> "It is absurd to be proud of one's ancestry—it is better to be an ancestor oneself."
>
> —Freud

So what have you orchestrated here
This memory of yours and its few particulars,
Old skin sitting and watching on television
A black man and shaking my head (*you* say)
As if that were strength? What is this nonsense?
I am speaking and I want you to listen.
Don't go making of me a myth. I am a man who lacked
Will. Rich I might have been
And had women. But I can tell you
I wasn't smart enough. Why do you invest me with
Significance? What do you look for grandson
With your eyes fixed so on the past? Don't reach
Back as if it were gold. Gold is gold.
The past is past.
       Don't make from my life art.
Even if you stumbled on something you would like
To call truth, what difference can it make?
I am as strange to myself
As my wife was to me, as I tried not to be
To my children, as I am to you. Here for you is poetry:
We are stars caught like prisoners in the sky. Defeat
Is everywhere. In the dirt under your fingernails.
       So what
If I hadn't come to America. I would have risen
With my children over Europe in smoke.
Listen. I am only the ash in your throat.
       When Kerensky
Rode up on that damned horse and called to me
As if he were a hero, I knew him
Goniff that he was. The Revolution? Ach, I heard
All of that and shit on such talk. They are thieves
All of them. He used me, and I him.
       Take Russia and
   America.
They chew you up like ignorance. The world is not of my
   making.
I am only what I became. Bitter?

No more. Yes I would have you know me. Almost
All my children are dead. The facts of my life have given up
Their light forever. Forever.
                         You want to know
Why I resisted coming to America? Read this, it is simple
Enough: Each morning before the sun I woke from my
        wife's side
Then walked to the end of town straight to my cousin's bed.
Make of that what you will. Don't make of it love.

So what if I return to you with stories. What difference
Can it make. When you are leaving and your children are
        taken
And your children's children as were my mother *there*
And my father dying with another wife here
Maybe then you will learn that forgetting is the law of life.
Maybe then you will come to know the arrogance of your
        art
And learn the beginning of humility.

Querying Death

When you are young death is a skyscraper and only as
you grow and time falls away like skin does he reveal
himself to be an old world tailor, so unassuming, so precise.

*

Death is the mother and father of Progress. Death may be
money in your pocket. Death will keep after you as if to
remind you the rent is due.

*

Death is a sweet pickle for poets and a pork barrel for
morticians.

*

Underneath your eyelids the canopy all in white, his
perfect and straight fingers are waving like flags in a May
breeze. The crowds press together to make benediction.
Death applauds like a child.

*

The *e* in death is a tenor vowel: pronounce the word fully
and with proper attention to texture: do you feel your teeth
cut into the soft plain of your tongue? Now, roll the tip
of your tongue onto the backside of your teeth and up into
the roof of your mouth. Suck into your throat. Now
swallow.

To the Failed Suicides

Finally you have returned.
You have walked back
Onto the narrows of your life.
Once more the shore has
Raised itself. Grasses root
Even in sand.
            This says nothing
About hope. What is dead remains dead—
And you have left something
Of your life behind.
            But you are back.
From the spaces where there are no walls,
Where words are like the rain
And hands have given up on gestures.

It is not that I claim privileged understanding.
If I have sat on more than one occasion
With my feet crossed and my fists
Tight like dead stone as if to keep the body
From crumbling, that is
No special knowledge. We have all been there.

But I have seen you pass in poor parade,
The soldiers of loss. I am no herald.
I cannot even begin to speak of victory.
What I can speak of is the blood
Riving its way in all things,
Rock, tree, weed, forever, the
Fingers, even, grabbing onto a rail overlooking
The city's panorama of lights,
Resisting the inexpressible pull of the earth's center.

Springtime Near Munich

On the 20th Anniversary of the Allies' liberation
of Dauchau, 1945-1965

"Ich bin du"
If This Is a Man, Primo Levi

1

It is a beautiful April morning.
The walk is banked
with purple crocuses
and the grass green
in the glare of sun. The
sunlight is almost shafting through the leaves.
The land is not rolling. There are no trees.
There are shiny spigots. They work
efficiently. As does the generator. And the traffic of bodies
peek-a-booing into corners, the clean ovens, the showers
dry. There are arms pinned with cut black ribbons—
they signify mourning. But there are gay
ribbons as well: it is the beginning of warmth once more.
Dressed for spring weather, the womens dresses
are printed with flowers; the mens faces are ashen. Somber.
Yellow armbands hang on invisible
arms limp like week old game. And
there are announcements tacked to walls: *Achtung!*
Prege, prege! Respectez
le silence. It is Sunday and church bells
splash through the breeze and the young girls
their hair ironed straight, silky black, blown
back gently like the flags of nations. This
is the desert the mind says. Deluxe black.
A cane comes click click-
ing mildly drunk, comic. Nails white, fingers scrubbed
palms surgical and red clapping
out teeth (thank you, may I have more sir) and others are
counting the gold. The barbers come with a flourish
of sirens. Four and twenty crows all
in a row. The air healthy and robust smelling of freshly cut
green.
No monument to heroes, a skeleton only
draped stupidly in folds of cement stands,

the memorial. (To what exactly?) And swaying beautifully
like a full-grown linden, the Hebrew wafts into the breeze
Adonai Eloheynu Adonai Echud
and the audience breaks bread,
flashbulbs light up and crack, serious lips blister
in the glare of heat. Pour wine now and eat the body of
remembrance. It is reported they
screamed themselves into silence, fouled themselves
and each other. And in each corner pieces
of flesh stick, stubbornly, to the wall. Corralled,
donkeys bray. The fleshy buttocks sweat   crowd
against the limp pricks; more buttocks
press helpless harder. Bellies soak.
Piss makes the floor slippery.
Ammonia stings the eyes. The screams are too loud
to hear. There is nowhere to fall
but up. There is the voyeur here? The
tongue hanging sitting in
the front row jamming tits in my
mouth. Leering into the showers. Showers. He runs his
finger down a wet crotch opens the
oven door and dives
into a ditch. Comes the click clicking. Clown.
The plow pushing bodies
steadily down the walk. Awaken. This is a trip.
You were not there. *Ich bin du.*
                                        You are.

                    2

Then is not now.
And now, sitting here,
is only a poem. Related they are
but how? Brothers? Father and son? The older
died each instant, the younger
lives on, more quietly,
as insufficient memory, as envelopes of facts,
as words which give voice to some
thing. Some anguish. A memory I was a visitor to only.

So what can it mean now
that almost fifteen years ago I entered

unknowingly into a carnival of mourning
(and was it unknowingly)?
What was it but some hours
in my life, hardly a moment
in the life of my children, and absurdly less
in that abstraction we call the earth's revolutions?
What can it mean
for my children who may never read
these lines, who, even if they do, may die
in ignorance, having grown up into the abstraction of
     America?

                                       1965, 1980

Breath

The dream was of rabbits
being pulled apart and
stacked like linen. The easy un-
dressing of fur by skilled hands like
a backbone pared from a young
fish. And the rabbits
were dead. And the
eyes stare as the mouth
moves—moved. Like nothing
less than a man dying and
needing more breath than the
arms of more than enough men willing
could shovel. And it was a
dream.

A Visit

If you listen and don't
turn away, you will hear
the blade in her voice
singing like a thief *free
me free me* and
                 leaving
the son of her body's
labor in pieces you will
hear—there is nothing
else you can do—the methodical
tearing away of
metaphor from her life.
The longing that is left
no more for beginnings but ends.

Long Beach

The time is one
of leavings. The sun as was once
believed burying down into the
earth. But needing
nowhere else to go, my
self in this room resides
with contentment. A man
who has no spaces left from his day
to fill. The ordinary
dissatisfactions have stacked themselves
neatly and in rows.
There are moments like now
when silence presses against the walls
and settles everywhere, into
each corner, when
the night's blackness is no metaphor.
Just black. And in its midst
I am in possession of the strength
we all crave. The sureness of oak.
The birch's suppleness. Neither power,
nor weakness. Nor appetites nor desires
nor loss. An ease with the sky's
blankness, the sea loud
(or call it dumb) and the earth,
possessing so much death, so much violence
and struggle gone to grain, so much
death from boredom.
                    It is not
that it does not matter. But like a bear
unexpectedly happening on a hive of honey
where, no doubt, there is danger, he accepts that.
Who knows if he is too greedy. My calm now
is no forgetting. It is a passing
that will go too soon. Like the Jews
who left city after city,
their luggage at hand always, their arrivals
always they must, in their hearts, have known,
temporary.

Running the Boardwalk

> "The whole power of the spirit is required
> for dying. . . ."
>   Kierkegaard

What do they recollect?
Their bodies sit like strangers outside
of themselves. In the
hot summer sun and the ocean
lifting its smell over the boardwalk railing
and into their dim orbit
they sit listening as if to the last
thirty years on transistor radios.
The canvas chairs sag
under that terrible shrinkage and my
legs carry on past
and speed up with the shameful pride of muscle
that is not so unequivocally
broken and that need to run, to feel
sweet pain. A stallion on an unbroken path
and clear.
                The sands burn
in the glare and the boardwalk
splinters its teak
flooring as the salt breeze rinses
my face. And the children
in all their nakedness and curls
as if the angels of death
on their shoulders were friends
of a lifetime. Run.
With such speed that the gull
sweeping above is the arm of the wind
carrying your body in flight past the old
Jews bundled against that glare, their suits
pressed, waiting, as if death
were a gentleman coming to escort them.
                                    What do they
think sitting there upright, kibbitzing, others
sitting so still they seem to have forgotten
to breathe. My God what is this empty
misery you have bundled

against the heat. As if the sun had need
of those dried bones. And run. Just run. Not
in a metaphor. Push. Against the weight
that these lungs have become.
Run. Into this death
seated like inmates waiting their last meal.

WPSY on Your Dial

Hello, this is Barbara, 28,
Do you hear me? Hello?
Am I on?
I'm scared, I'm still trying though.
What can I do?

> *Of course you're scared. You have*
> *Shaky legs. The foundation rocks.*

I was just wondering, that's all.

> *Good Barbara. Wonder is good. Just*
> *Don't forget the strengths*
> *You've acquired in therapy.*
> *Do you remember three things*
> *You learned? Can you recite them?*

I am *me* is one. My mistakes are no different
Than the president's or the Pope's is a second.
And a third is, take two valium,
One on rising and one at the dead of night.

> *Good for you Barbara. You*
> *Are growing. Don't forget*
> *Your inner light.*

Hello this is Dave, 26.
Hello, I am Chris. I am 27.
I am in a potential extramarital situation.
I'd like you to help me with the anxiety
I am likely to encounter there.
It first arrived the other night, precisely at 12:20 a.m.
While I was eating spinach quiche.
What should I do?
Should I or should I not?

> *Walk into the wardrobe of fear Chris*
> *And observe yourself. Listen to the wonder of your heart*
> *And work on your feelings. Deal*
> *With them. As you would*
> *With a king and the ace of spades.*

30

Thank you doctor. Listen, I saw you this
Morning on the Morning Show and
You are quite attractive. Doctor
I wonder . . .

Good afternoon, you're next on WPSY.

Hello, I am Theresa, aged 24.
I don't know what to do.
Please, I don't know. I know only
That I am angry and cannot keep it back.

> *I can understand your anger, Theresa.*
> *I have been there myself*
> *And have come back to say, don't*
> *Turn off the faucets.*

I feel like the foundation has fallen away.
I am upset. Oh doctor, I am scared.

> *I can understand your being scared.*
> *I have been scared. It takes a lot, Theresa, to say*
> *I am scared. But we all do make mistakes.*
> *Are you willing to work on it? You*
> *And he will have to deal with it,*
> *Theresa. Is he willing to work and deal?*
> *If he is coming back for forgiveness*
> *And if he is willing to work*
> *On it, deal.*

Hello, this is Bob, 42. I am angry also
But, doctor, I am unable to let it show.

> *How can you constructively act out your anger, Bob.*
> *I recommend two things: counseling, and you*
> *Will enjoy life much more, and you must learn to say*
> *It is all right to be angry. I would*
> *Recommend assertiveness training*
> *Where you can learn to stand firm. If you*
> *Have further problems, read* Creative Aggression
> *And in 45 days you will be home free home.*

Hello, I am Michael, 24.
I push and push against the tide
But I am having a communications
Problem. She doesn't seem
To see her mistakes
When I point them out to her.

> *Do you love her Michael? Do*
> *You cherish and honor her?*
> *Is there enough foreplay? Or are you*
> *A selfish male*
> *Intent only on your own excited itch?*

Hello, this is Margaret, age 45.
I want to be emotionally available
For another relationship.

> *Oh Margaret, be honest with yourself,*
> *For if to your ownself you*
> *Are not, then you may not be opening yourself*
> *For availability. . . .*

Hello, this is Robert, 22. Hello this is Dick
Age 45 and life is not what I expected.
Hello this is Jane age 45 and
My dog Spot died and I am suicidal. Hello. Hello.

Partly Pandemonium, Partly Love

I love great men I love. Nobody's great.
I must remember that.

1

"Daddy where's the moon I want the moon"

Berryman dead. If I could
I would cry. My son has been crying.
Afraid? I don't know. We neither of us
Can say; we mourn in our different ways,
Him (I might imagine) for the moon
And I for . . . Berryman is dead
And it is meaningless to you. It is
Almost meaningless for me. Shhhh
The moon is asleep. She will come
But it is a long trip and she needs her rest.
We must wait. Come, lay down,
I'll make you a song

> *Down down the moon fell down*
> *She was wearing an old maid's gown.*
> *Pulled up high, zipped up tight*
> *Nobody sleeps with her tonight.*

Shhh, don't cry. There is nothing to
Be frightened of. There are no ghosts. I am here.
Come, we'll crayon our own moon. Shhhh
Bridges are washing away in the rain and
She may be a long time coming.

2

The poets die. And we read the memorials; the
Obituaries prepared well in advance, follow.
And what have we left for ordinary men, drunks, poor
Slobs, soldiers, good family men and bad, whores,
Social workers, all the rest dying
Singly and by dozens, thousands,
Masses like no metaphor can describe. What, finally, do we
     say? It is
Necessary to forget and we do and our memories are like
Yesterday's news. And it is necessary. In face of

33

Bayonets that do what bombs have left undone; in
Face of murder, riots, jails, hunger that makes
The knuckles raw, floods, tidal waves—there is no
Bridge high enough.
                              It is the new year; the old
Has not been left behind. Loss
Inhabits eyes that are dry. But we have poems. You write
Something. And then? Those who call
Themselves poet, what is a poet?
Poems are make believe. Are poets?
Berryman dead. Kenneth Patchen whose work
I don't know well, whose looks have been crippled
So long has died today. He is survived by wife
And many poems. What do sentiments mean?
Delmore Schwartz. Dead six years now?
Now Berryman, burned-out ego, poet whose
Poems I've loved, what has survived you? The hordes
Walk every day non-stop into cadavers, in Bengal, Vietnam,
Africa, in America my home. These
Words, these silly words which only for a moment
Ground the madness, which only in a fiction build
Bridges high enough to cross, these inky marks
Only waste their time in a man's life because   because
Why? Answers
John Berryman-O, Henry
Pussycat. What are they but a minstrel show,
Where blackface hides the shrapnel and the coal
And bridges are a mass of paste and gaudy colors.
They cannot hold. In my bed, not insomniac, but wide awake
I make my fiction.
                              There you are, peeking from
The curtain. Your cue. You tip-toe out, stealthing, be-
Hind your beard, smirking like a kid. You
Stand there hairy-legged, naked (with black socks)
In the snow, waving to all us fans out here
In the fourth row. The sign says you are leaving
On a grand trip—the player-piano hits
Some kinky notes. We applaud, you wave good-bye, and

Are off (the sign now says) to see Delmore, Randall,
Ted, all that un-merry gang living
Somewhere in a bunch of poems. We sit applauding
And the curtain falls.

"Your letter warmed a chilly day. . . . Delmore
is not forgotten."

I have worked through the night
Until the words have been emptied
Of breath. Dead lungs they are.
An old drunk in a corner
Slopped in urine. Stop. It
Is late and I am looking
Too hard for metaphor. It is too late too
To sleep now. I have been sitting
Here uncomfortable, sticking pins in my eyes
For tears. I am tired but not
Sleepy; I am neither afraid nor unafraid.
Colloidal suspension chemists might say.
Time magazine has condensed this week's casualties,
All those bodies, not only Vietnam, not only Bangladesh,
Those bodies slopped in mud, eyeless, pieces
And broken bits of grimace, that
Feast of burned and broken bones. Tears? Anger?
Are they enough? Toast the dead to pandemonium.
Berryman has made Milestones: fifteen lines (and
Four of them quotation). Lowell will get a
Larger spread. Roethke rocked in drink listens
To the wind, and all that gang is waiting
For the Man. Only Delmore is deep in sleep.
This is a fine night, a fine fine night, making
Poems to wake the dead.

May Morning Rain

For days it seems, the rains have kept ticking with steady
precision, drowning all sounds—even the birds out here—
and settling must everywhere like an enormous and
permanent presence, in the sheets, the empty spaces of
this page, the dark earth full and breathing. Before me
and I suppose I will see this each year as if always for the
first time, this rich green is overgrowing, you could say,
willfully, uncontained. It is what you will miss most, this
passion riving through every cell, of every living thing.
It will not give up. Call this a parable of need: not letting
go, returning each time from what appeared to be the end.
I think of my poor mother, dead so long now her memory
ministers only silence. But it is there and if you could
hear it, the sound would be like rivers driving seams in the
earth, roiling through every obstacle like life itself. This
is the passion of love. And it never gives up.

The Fire of Love

With a friend of mine, when I was younger and raw, we
were in a cocktail lounge and I was for no reason drinking
deeply. Next to us at a small table three older women sat—
I said something to one of them, about what I don't
remember now, and continued drinking and was soon
taken by her large, I could imagine, aged breasts and dark
starry nipples, getting hot, beginning to imagine and know-
ing inside the small chilled fear of ignorance. My friend
John Kreutzer may not remember any of this but he sat
back, detached, amazed at my doggy drive ("A duck
would have been good enough" he said the next day and
also, with a cockeyed smile, that he left because he was
in my way). And she I persisted with and the woman's
friends (travellers from Missouri) got up to "turn in"
asking her to come—she hedged and they said good night,
coolly, or so it seemed. And we had another drink and
another and I must have spun something, how I don't
know, and left shortly after, me with the scent (and scared)
of victory and I do remember us climbing the stairs to my
second floor motel room, me next to and behind coaxing
her up and getting her inside and my drunk mouth finding
hers, tugging the long zipper at her back down, with no
tact at all, pulled at her, hedged and girdled in, the bras-
siere with too many snaps, my 22-year old prick so hot
it couldn't wait and before I knew anything—and I knew
little—was inside her, so hot and drunk, so unknowing
and . . . that poor woman. What must she have needed?
But I never thought, only sobered, too soon, and seeing
that old hag as she was, her valleys having drifted out in
all their terrible clarity, her tits hanging as if overripe, and
her wanting something—she must have—which I didn't
know or think to give and, even if I did, was too young
and stupid and gone. She wanted to spend the night.
Sobriety took hold and I grabbed hold, forcing her to get
her girdle on, her brassiere and slip and pushing her out
almost as hard as I pushed her up and embarrassed like
hell. Not for her as I should have been—but for myself.
For myself.

And what makes me think tonight of that youthful stupid-
ity? It is not the smug victory. In all these years I have not

thought about that, not once, and until tonight have never
felt shame nor thought to. Never honest to god thought
of her. And now, I don't feel guilt as much as I feel for
that woman if she is even still alive and for whatever good
it can do. It has brought me back. I sat next to a dear
friend tonight at Jim Wright's poetry reading and watched
her mouth and all the years that have crowded into her
body as if for one night they could be friends, and watched
her aging beauty and wanted to love her, as a lover, know-
ing—not for lack of wanting—I could never be enough.
And watched her rich-veined hands hold onto themselves,
unable to stop, those mad fingers in all their passion going
for each other, not getting enough of themselves and
desired that woman as if I were man enough to bring her
back to love and know once more the fire of love.

Poetry

There are some memories that will
never give you up; like disaster
they hold on as if they had no
other reason. Even when they seem

to have abandoned you, when you
think you have done with them and
their every sensation. And when the time
comes and it does and you feel everything

has been emptied from you forever and
even your rage has turned to a dull
violence and you see with every disbelief
your father's face listening in the mirror

you will still need them and you will
come in all your poverty seeking and
like the children you could never
abandon they will return from nowhere

dragging you back
and you will know you are all right.

II

"One day as I was coming home from school, suddenly a big bubble! A big bubble stopped in front of me. It wrapped itself around me and we went floating. Late that night we were over the Atlantic Ocean. We came into Scotland, then England, then France. Then we floated back to Canada where my mother and father were. I popped the balloon and fell into my father's arms."

*　　　　　*　　　　　*

"All you want to do is throw me around."

Blessings

It is my desire for fruit, you es-
pecially, your tart pulp jibbing
my taste   your rich
smell running windward on
my tongue curved like
a spinnaker its taste full of
seed splitting the curve
of the rind breaking
fruit. Your taste   the
quince and green space and
marvel of tartness.
                    Says the
goat laughing   friend, it's the high blue
and spring

2

The morning sparkles like lemons
and I am carrying the
gifts of seed   apples   figs   pears
especially pears pregnant
seedy   full   that
the tongue licking a jug of honey
rocks in delight with and
oranges and grapes purpling
lips and a man who
cares for the deep yellow   who
loves the feel
the firm and the round of a pear and eats

Hands

Each morning you wake
and the hands take hold
as they are taking hold all
over the world opening *Pravda* and
The Minneapolis Times, cracking open
jumbo eggs in Las Vegas, patting
the heads of children off to school.
The hands that took you into this life
are uprooting great oaks are
cutting bread in the morning light
are the hands chipping at the dark
bone of mountains underground
are the hands steering like cattle
through traffic.
                    Look at these hands
with their rich relations. With their
fingers trekking like pioneers
over breasts, moving recklessly
into caves—these millions
of hands desiring so, these hands
wringing their anguish at
soap operas, mindlessly smacking the
child, exchanging money. And what clowns!
Watch them imitate barking dogs
or sneak through alleys like rats.
These marvellous hands—what gives them
such versatility, walking erect like
princes one year, wandering the next
like drunks. What gives them
their love of craft? of hysteria? of
self-pity?
                    Oh these hands, crying
or rejoicing
like tongues deep in the juice
of this earth, dancing like Shiva
as if lost into time. Oh
applaud these hands. Applaud.

A Snub for Mr. and Ms. Exegesis

"The only way," he says, "is with me,
King Silver (plate)." And he sits up
tall and says, "fellow friends I
am your entrance into the spectral
fat of white." And Mr. Blue (who worked
the railroad) sat up and cheered; and
Mrs. Orange wept fat orangy tears and even
her old maid sister Miss Yellow
sat simply (with a crocked smile). All
except old Missus Green her
hair sprouting seed up
stairs screaming, "You
know you know the winter
is not black, not gray—
and there is no white. My
friends, my dear friends (you
are going to
hell) won't some

body love me?"

October Weather

My son says, "the trees are angry"—
the wind says so too. The
leaves have lost
their tough. They don't need
this aggravation. They don't
need to be told.
                    The squirrel
lies in its blank curl still
hugging the branch. The
little emerald buzzards still dance, still
split more skin, methodic-
ally feast upon this feast.

Inner Weather

It is a morning of masquerade,
as if these last days
of October could
counterfeit blossoms and
new birth and sap
heavy with slowness
and moving.

If you are with
me walking through these
banks of leaves you
are still gone. And I am bereft.
There is no other
way to say it.

So how shall I come to you?
With what metaphors? The clouds
do not darken. There are
no terrible rains. If all
manner of birds are leaving
south, as many stay.

There is nothing
out here that says you are gone.
And everything.

Poem in January

Bent over
there he cries,
all the seed
of his manhood in him.
I think he has come on his
weaknesses too soon.
And I grieve for him.
There is something we both know
is inconsolable, no matter
how much of his body I can still
contain in my arms. My
ministrations are of no use. This
picture is as engraved in
my blood as in yours.

It is morning and
I am driving east. The sun
while it has not yet shown itself
has, as we say, started up. The graying clouds
are scraped in swatches
of fierce orange. All over the world, even
down the country roads off this highway
men and women in the most inconsolable ways
are dying wholly unprepared. That
has nothing and everything to do.

In Rousseau's picture
Le Parc des Buttes Chaumont
a child carrying a hoop and holding
his father's hand, the mother ahead,
walk deep into the black forest serene.
                                       Ahead
the red tail lights are disappearing into the gray
morning. The cold splindly limbs speed by
as if in a stalled clamor.

What is this here?
What other poems have remembered
thousands and thousands of times
over. The grief that sits there, as if

it had no beginning, that was known
even before knowledge began.
                              We know
the ending. We know we know
and still the sun is as we say rising
beginning

Grief

There is nothing
That delivers its wound
With the same ease
As your child's mad words.

They feed on you
Like a sleek crow driven
With angry lust
In his beak.

He gnaws at your heart.
Pecks with his grief.
Fattens himself, helplessly
And still feeds and feeds

As if he knew nothing
Of being satiated.
Here he is, your one-time
Self. Your gift. Your grief.

Lunch

I know there is nothing of abiding love
In this—we are not talking of
Making over our lives. What we might have
Become we already are.
Sitting across from each other
I accept that and I expect
You do. It's what we don't talk of,
There, under the awning, separated
By the gleaming white cloth fluttering its wings,
The only ones. About us,
Bodies hurrying or simply moving
With the chilly Spring aimlessness. Rain is
Hovering, clouds you might imagine wandering
Like caravans. We are served. Our waitress
Not hurrying, in a yellow scarf
Smiles like a warm breeze trembling through buds
Not yet opened.
          The sailboats
Across the way are rocking in their perches.
The soup heavy, holding its warmth, the
Bread thick and spongy. The pure pleasure
Here and nothing else.
There are these moments I swear
Of perfection. They have been known
I know since the first erect animals
Stopped to gaze at the world
About them and for a moment forgot
About fear and hunting and being hunted
And heard, maybe not even then for the
First time, songs of praise and gratefulness
Trembling through their bodies.

The Gift

Of fathers and
sons there is the
impossibility.
They stand on
decks gripping
each others' arms; or
fending off. Their
eyes stray
with the shame of young lovers.
Between them words
are the poor dancers who blundered.
And in your lost presence friend when
I have been careless of my son's one life
and have glimpsed your own
irrevocable loss walk-
ing like a blind man between
cars and your arms
flailing with the grace of wings broken
by something outside your
control can I
remember to thank creation for all
her wizardry and lack
of it and know my son's one life
a gift as much mine as his.

Rising

The poem I thought was in the memory as it rose again,
involuntarily, like a child's need for love. But I was only
partly right; for the poem is in that mystery of need, as
this morning, in its coming towards me, here (if I say,
"in greeting" or "warning" that is untrue), then off again,
but always, always, in the field of return. And I love that
need and love its necessity as with your own child when
a madness is on him and refuses to let go and he is beyond
all reason bereft, your hands take his body to yours and
the sun's tide rises in you again and again and again.

Penelope (Who Fed Me Prunes and Oatmeal)

I once began this poem:

"for one moment tonight
i stared at my fingers
& could not believe their size.
from what did i grow, from
where? she is some fiction
i have made into a penelope,
some intimate fancy of mind."

And then followed, "i have heard
crows caw-cawing in the barn,
bats and field mice caught up,
their bones cracking like dry
sticks in an august blaze."

I wrote all this and
witness now that it is untrue. Should
I have known then?

"i have heard her called gentle," yes;
but I have heard, as well, other
ridiculous things
that were either untrue
or irrelevant or dumb. "in her lodged
a seed," yes; "grown, fed, comforted," yes; but
"wrinkled, ill-weaned, grown to
proportions monstrous, hounding
her grave [I must have been
reading *Wuthering Heights*] to leave
stones that are swept
away from one winter to the next"? No

no—I am big, not monstrous; I do not hound
her grave, but visit (not very regularly); and follow-
ing custom—for some reason or other—leave stones
that, from one visit to the next, sometimes
remain and sometimes do not.

On the Chattahoochee River

Now I have known as well as
anyone here that the river is no longer a god,
that that is poetry getting drunk on itself.
I know the travel agents have their mitts in it,
that it is a thoroughfare for the chamber of commerce,
for the unions and politicians, that
they are leaving their sewage eating into the banks,
that behind the dark green kudzo
cities and towns are silting like stumps
into a savage boredom.
And except for what you can manage to save
and to rail against in your own house,
that is America
franchising itself to hell. I know

the river is no god. I know
and know that its miles and miles of imagination
are uninhabited except for a small
turbulence here and there, call it a sand bar,
a turtle dropping off a log, a poem up and
leaping, the current tugging as if it had
its own needs and somewhere to get to.

In the Mountains
Grantsville, Maryland

Letting the screen door collapse against
the frame; leaving the gray
glow of the television and our son's
slivvering cry, the mouse's poor breaths
that will struggle in the dark full sink later
when we sleep, and
out into the nightcave
for no simple reason. The moon
has been carried away and the two
remaining stars emptied of light.
Fear is waiting beyond and down
the hill, in the impenetrable black,
deep in the high wild grass beside
the mountain laurel, the timothy, the
oats; my feet naked and tentative
squish through the drenched mud. They
are afraid to hold too tight,
want light, yet move
against reason into what
corners, what lostness, wanting
something.
          We are in the country
of our choosing—exiles still
in these spaces that belong completely
to themselves. The dark is no invader—this
is its land. And with no television glow,
no child's blonde head to comfort, no book to
free your mind from the color of death,
having only the uncertain strange sounds
in this jaw of night,
fearing your own ignorance
you are here, only, and
the terrible fear of your own fear.
And if you will only push against
reason, if you will only lay down against your own
reason, deep into the dark
grass you will feel the wetness

wrap its cold fingers about your buttocks,
the nails harden your nipples, the
chill riding its way through you
and the morning's step
as it slowly and deliberately walks
over the red lips of hills.

Take Hold

If there is nothing
before you, take hold
of it. You may be fortunate
or not. Place it deep
in your pocket regardless.
It is a possession,
as no other.

When you are to leave and
have made all your
preparations; when you
are ordered to declare all
your possessions, reach in
to the dark pocket.

This is a symbol
traveller, a parable
perhaps. Nothing
is as whole as the
space in the air
you pass through.
And it is yours. If
you will take hold of it.

Cover design by Susan Foster

Partly Pandemonium, Partly Love was composed by
Barbara Shaw at The Writer's Center Bookworks
(Glen Echo Park, Maryland). The typeface is
Compugraphic English Times and is based on
Stanley Morison's Times Roman. One thousand
copies have been printed for Dryad Press on Warren
Olde Style (an acid-free paper) by Thompson-Shore,
Inc. Two hundred fifty have been bound in boards,
the first fifty numbered and signed.

Merrill Leffler was born in 1941 in Brooklyn, New York. He received a degree in physics and for six years was an engineer before leaving to do graduate study in literature. After three years at St. Catherine's College, Oxford, he returned to the United States in 1972 to do further graduate work and teach in the English departments of the University of Maryland and the U.S. Naval Academy. In 1967 he and Neil Lerhman started *Dryad* magazine and, in 1974, Dryad Press. He has worked as a free-lance writer, his articles and reviews appearing in *The New Republic*, the *Washington Post Book World*, the *Christian Science Monitor*, *Mosaic* (the National Science Foundation), *Washington Review*, and *Baltimore Sun*. He is currently with Maryland Sea Grant, writing about biological and environmental research on Chesapeake Bay. He lives in Takoma Park, Maryland, with his wife Ann Slayton and two children, Jeremy and Daniel.

Books from Dryad Press

Roger Aplon, *Stiletto*
Denis Boyles, *Maxine's Flattery*
Ann Darr, *Cleared for Landing*
Frank Dwyer, *Looking Wayward*
Roland Flint, *Say It*
Marguerite Harris, ed., *A Tumult for John Berryman*
Philip K. Jason, ed. *Shaping: New Poems in Traditional Prosodies*
Philip K. Jason, *Thawing Out*
Rod Jellema, *The Lost Faces*
Rodger Kamenetz, *The Missing Jew*
Barbara Lefcowitz, *The Wild Piano*
Merrill Leffler, *Partly Pandemonium, Partly Love*
Neil Lehrman, *Perdut (a novel)*
John Logan, *Poem in Progress*
Linda Pastan, *On the Way to the Zoo* (2nd printing)
Linda Pastan, *Setting the Table* (letterpress and trade)
Myra Sklarew, *From the Backyard of the Diaspora* (new edition)
Susan Sonde, *Inland is Parenthetical*
Sidney Sulkin, *The Secret Seed* (stories and poems)
Reed Whittemore, *The Feel of Rock: Poems of Three Decades*
Irving Wilner, *Poems of the Later Years*
James Wright, *Moments of the Italian Summer* (2nd printing)
Paul Zimmer, *With Wanda: Town & Country Poems*

Send for descriptive catalog